WHAT IS JUDAISM?

WRITTEN BY
SHARI LAST

BEING JEWISH

What does it mean to be Jewish?

Judaism is not a religion, ethnicity, or culture. It is a combination of all these things and more.

Thousands of years ago, there were 12 Israelite tribes in the ancient land of Judah (or Judea). There, they developed practices and spiritual beliefs that were closely tied to the land. The collection of laws, beliefs, and traditions of the people of Judah is known as Judaism.

The descendants of these tribes from Judah — who continue these traditions today, wherever they live — are the Jewish people.

THE TORAH
Judaism centers around the belief in a single God and the observance of His laws, which are written in the Torah — the Jewish bible, or holy book.

Nowadays, there are many types of Jews. Some of them strictly follow the ancient laws of the Torah. Some of them keep a few of the traditions. Some of them don't. Some of them believe in God. Some don't. Some live in Israel. Some don't.

The only thing all Jewish people have in common is that their ancestors came from the Israelite tribes of the land of Judah.

ARE YOU READY TO FIND OUT MORE ABOUT JUDAISM?

WHAT DO JEWISH PEOPLE BELIEVE?

Jewish people believe there is one God who created everything. They believe He knows everything, and that He is good.

According to Judaism, the Torah (the Hebrew bible) was written by God. It contains the history and laws of the Jewish people. By following the Jewish laws, a Jew will honor God, become a better person, and help make the world a better place.

While Jews believe that God is all-knowing and all-powerful, they also believe He gives humans free will to choose our own actions.

WHO IS THE JEWISH GOD?

The Jewish God has many names, and some are so holy they are not meant to be spoken out loud! Most of God's names are only to be uttered during prayer, which is why most Jewish people simply call God "HaShem" — which means "the name".

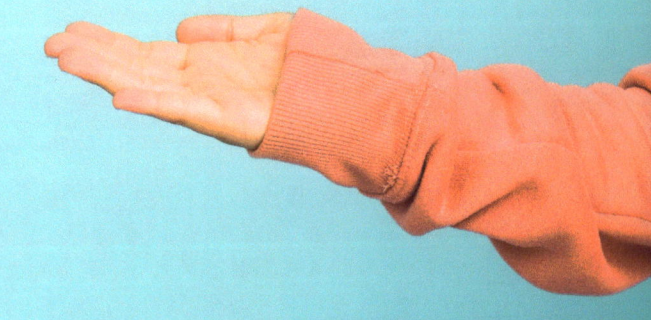

It's important to remember that not all Jews are the same and they don't all think or believe the same things. Some Jews don't believe in God, some choose to practice other religions, and some choose not to call themselves Jewish. The rest of this book refers to Jewish people who embrace Judaism as part of their identity.

WHAT DO JEWISH PEOPLE DO?

Most Jewish people do the same things as you! They eat, go to school, go to work, talk to their friends, read books, play video games, look after their pets, ride bikes, spend time with their families, celebrate special occasions, go on holiday, give to charity, volunteer, enjoy sleepovers, and watch TV. As well as all this, many Jews include Jewish practices and traditions in their everyday life.

SHABBAT

Every Saturday, Jews observe Shabbat. This is a day of rest. Many Jews go to synagogue on Shabbat, eat special meals with their families, and keep the laws of Shabbat. We will learn more about Shabbat in a few pages!

PRAYER

The Torah says that Jews should pray three times each day — in the morning, afternoon, and evening. Some Jews pray at home on their own, others go to synagogue. Some pray all three times, some don't, and some don't pray at all.

KEEPING KOSHER

Kosher describes the foods that Jewish people are allowed to eat. There are many rules about this, and we will learn about some of them later on this book!

TYPES OF JEWS

Jews originate from Judah (Judea, which was in a similar place to modern-day Israel), but most of them were expelled from there around 2,500–3,000 years ago. Since then, they have lived and built communities all around the world.

DIFFERENT PLACES

Over time, different groups developed unique cultural traditions that became entwined with their Judaism. Some of the largest groups of Jews are:

Mizrahi — Middle East and North Africa
Sephardi — Spain and Portugal
Ashkenazi — Europe
Ethiopian — Ethiopia

DIFFERENT PRACTICES

Even within these groups, people practice their Judaism in different ways. For example, secular Jews don't observe the religious laws (or maybe just a few of them), whereas traditional Jews preserve the major customs. Orthodox Jews stick closely to the rules of the Torah, while Reform Judaism offers a more modern form of the religion.

Although there are many "strands" of Judaism, some people don't identify with any of these groups, some identify with more than one, and many fall somewhere in between!

SHABBAT

Shabbat is the Jewish day of rest. According to the Torah, God created the world in six days. On the seventh day, He rested – and so do we!

Shabbat begins at sundown on Friday night and ends after sunset on Saturday (25 hours in total). On Shabbat, Jewish people generally go to synagogue, eat meals with family and friends, and relax.

SHABBAT RULES

The Torah lists 39 activities that are considered "work", and which are therefore not allowed on Shabbat. These include writing, cooking, and baking, as well as activities that were more common in biblical times, such as weaving, ploughing, and lighting fires.

Since then, rabbis have used this list to outline modern actions that would also be considered "work". These include:
- Turning electricity on or off
- Driving
- Conducting business

This means going to work, shopping, driving, drawing, cooking, and using electronic devices are not permitted on Shabbat. (Weaving, ploughing, lighting fires, and all 39 of the original forms of work are also still forbidden!)

This doesn't mean Jewish people sit in the dark on Shabbat and eat raw food! It just means they need to plan in advance. Food is cooked before Shabbat. Lights are left on in advance (or set on a timeswitch). People walk instead of drive and talk or play instead of watching TV. It's actually a very enjoyable, social day!

A SHABBAT DAY . . .

CANDLE LIGHTING

Shabbat begins at sunset on Friday. There are very specific timings for this and they can be found on Jewish calendars. Women light Shabbat candles to welcome in the day of rest. Some light two candles, while others light one for each member of their family.

FAMILY MEALS

There are two main Shabbat meals: Friday night dinner and Shabbat lunch. Many families invite guests. I enjoy eating meals with cousins or family friends, but some weeks, it's just my own family, and those are fun too!

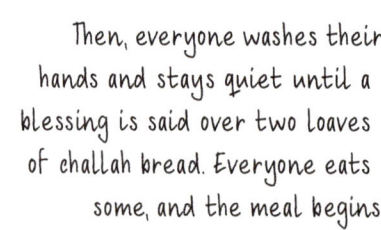

KIDDUSH

The meals start with a blessing over wine (or grape juice), which is known as kiddush.

Then, everyone washes their hands and stays quiet until a blessing is said over two loaves of challah bread. Everyone eats some, and the meal begins.

CHALLAH

JEWISH DAYS

In Judaism, a day begins when the sun sets and lasts until sunset the following day. Shabbat and festivals always begin in the evening and continue the next day.

SYNAGOGUE

On Shabbat, many more Jewish people go to synagogue than during the week. (This is because they go to work or school and can't always make it to synagogue in the week!) Shabbat morning is the main service, which generally lasts 2-3 hours and includes prayers and a reading of the weekly Torah portion. My synagogue has a children's service where younger kids sing songs and learn Torah stories.

HAVDALAH

Shabbat ends after the sun sets on Saturday. To mark the change from holy day to regular day, we say a prayer called Havdalah. During Havdalah, we hold a candle and smell sweet spices, such as cloves, mint, or cinnamon.

KEEPING KOSHER

There are two main laws for keeping kosher:

1. Only certain animals are kosher.

2. You cannot mix meat foods with dairy foods.

In addition, kosher food must be prepared with kosher utensils and cooked in kosher ovens. So if a meal contains all kosher ingredients but is cooked in a non-kosher oven, it is not kosher!

DID YOU KNOW?

Because Jewish people don't mix milk and meat, a kosher kitchen generally has two sets of everything (plates, cutlery, pots – sometimes even sinks and dishwashers), using one for meat and one for dairy. Some even have a third set for "parev" food, which is neither meat nor dairy, such as fruit or pasta.

WHAT ABOUT NATURAL FOODS?

Natural foods with no added ingredients, such as fruits, vegetables, flour, eggs, rice, spices, etc., are kosher.

WHAT MAKES AN ANIMAL KOSHER?

Mammals: must chew the cud and have split hooves
Fish: must have fins and scales
Birds: must be listed in the Torah as kosher

CAN YOU EAT DAIRY *AFTER* MEAT?

No. After eating meat, you need to wait a certain amount of time before eating dairy so the meat can be digested. Some people have a custom to wait 6 hours, some wait 3, and some wait 1. BUT . . . dairy is digested much quicker than meat so most people agree you *can* eat meat after dairy as long as you rinse your mouth out in between!

HOW DO YOU KNOW WHAT'S KOSHER?

In places with large Jewish communities, there will often be kosher butchers, bakeries, and shops. In addition, many countries have a "kashrut authority" that creates a list of specific foods and brands that are authorized as kosher in that country – such as bread, milk, coffee, crisps, and chocolate.

EVERYDAY LIFE

During a regular day, there are many Jewish things to do. For example, saying a blessing each time you eat, wearing certain items of clothing, kissing a mezuzah as you go through a door, or reciting the Shema prayer at bedtime.

MITZVAHS

A mitzvah is a commandment from the Torah, such as praying to God, saying a blessing before you eat, respecting your parents, eating kosher, helping others, and being honest. It is good to do a mitzvah! There are 613 commandments in the Torah. Most people probably do a few mitzvahs in their everyday lives without even realizing it!

BLESSINGS

There are a lot of blessings in Judaism! There's a blessing when you wake up (to thank God for letting us wake up), blessings before and after you eat, blessings after going to the toilet, for seeing a rainbow, for going on long journeys, for surviving danger, and a blessing to say before going to bed.

MEZUZAH

Jewish people hang a mezuzah on their doorposts. It is a container with a scroll inside. The scroll contains a prayer, the "Shema", and is meant to protect the people inside the house. Some Jews kiss the mezuzah whenever they pass through the doorway.

PRAYING

Many Jews pray every day, facing toward Jerusalem. (Some pray up to three times a day.) You can pray at synagogue or at home by yourself. Lots of different prayers are recited and they can be found in a Jewish prayer book called a siddur. Some prayers praise God, others ask Him to heal the sick, protect the Jewish people, forgive us for doing wrong, rebuild the Holy Temple, and bring peace to the world.

CLOTHING

There are a few special items of clothing that Jewish people might wear every day. Some boys and men wear a kippah — a head covering — as well as tzitzit, a fringed garment, under their clothes. These remind us of God and His commandments.

WHAT DO JEWISH KIDS LEARN IN SCHOOL?

Jewish schools teach regular subjects — such as reading, writing, math, science, geography, history — alongside Jewish subjects. All schools are different of course, but at my school we learn about the Jewish holidays, Torah stories of Jewish history, Jewish values, and how to do lots of mitzvahs. We also pray every morning and learn to read and write Hebrew so we can learn directly from the Torah.

THE STORY OF THE JEWS

The Torah contains the laws of Judaism, and it also records the first part of Jewish history. Of course, this history has continued since biblical times, and is still being written today! Let's take a look at the origins of the Jewish people.

FIRST JEW
Abraham was the first Jew. He, his son Isaac, and grandson Jacob, are the three "fathers" of Judaism. Instructed by God, Abraham moved his family to the land of Canaan. God promised that they would become a great nation in that land.

GROWING NATION
Jacob's 12 sons became known as the 12 tribes of Israel (Israel was another name given to Jacob). Their descendants went to Egypt and were enslaved there for 210 years.

FINDING FREEDOM
Moses became leader of the Israelites and demanded that Pharaoh release them from slavery. God struck Egypt with 10 plagues, until the slaves were freed. After crossing the Red Sea, the tribes received the Ten Commandments and the Torah at Mount Sinai.

THE PROMISED LAND
The Israelites wandered in the Sinai desert for 40 years, before arriving at the promised land. Each of the 12 tribes lived in their own area and eventually they became the United Kingdom of Israel under the first king, Saul. Theys built their communities according to the laws of the Torah.

JEWISH TEMPLES
The third king, Solomon, built a Temple in Jerusalem, within the kingdom of Judah. The Temple was destroyed around 400 years later by the invading Babylonians. A second Temple was built but also destroyed, this time by the conquering Romans, who renamed the area Judea, after the kingdom of Judah.

EXILE FROM THE LAND
After the destruction of the Temples, Jews were taken as slaves or exiled from Judea. Since then, there was no Jewish homeland – until the modern state of Israel was re-established in 1948.

A JEWISH HOME

You might walk into a Jewish person's house and think it looks like any other house. And many of them do! However, some Jewish homes will have small differences, which show how the people who live there bring their Judaism into their everyday life.

WALLS

Many Jewish people display Jewish art on their walls.

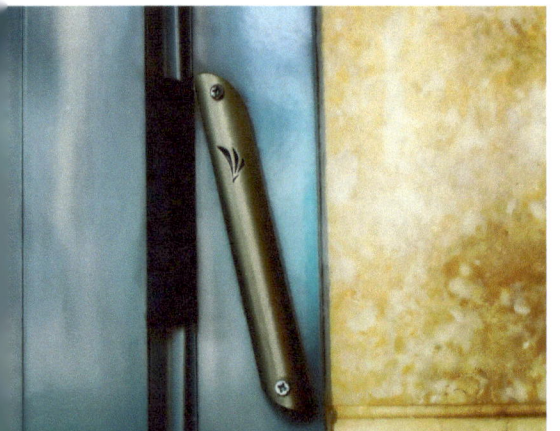

DOORS

Jewish people hang mezuzahs on their doorposts (every room, apart from the bathroom).

KITCHEN

Those who keep kosher will have a way of keeping their meat and dairy foods separate. Some have two sinks!

LIVING ROOM

A lot of Jewish homes will have Jewish books on their bookshelves.

HALLWAY

Some Jews hang up a home blessing in their front hallway.

JEWISH VALUES

The Torah contains the laws of Judaism, but it also includes stories and wisdom that teach a way of life. Jewish values are learned by studying the Torah and the writings of rabbis and other wise people, who comment on the Torah. These are some of the fundamental Jewish values:

- BELIEF IN ONE GOD
- TRUTH AND JUSTICE
- RESPECT FOR ELDERS
- KINDNESS
- CELEBRATING LIFE
- NOT SPEAKING BADLY OF OTHERS
- STRIVING TO BE A BETTER PERSON

THE VALUE OF CURIOSITY

Judaism values education and debate. Children and adults are always encouraged to ask questions, discuss different points of view, and look deeper into small details.

TZEDAKAH

Tzedaka means "charity". The word comes from *tzedek*, the Hebrew word for "justice". Jewish people are encouraged to give money to charity, as well as donating their time and efforts when they can to help others.

TIKKUN OLAM

This means "changing/improving the world". Jewish people are encouraged to actively work to make the world a better place. This can be in a small personal way like helping a friend, but it can extend to volunteering within your community, or further to include working for social justice.

CONNECTION TO ISRAEL

Judaism has always had a fundamental connection to the land of Israel, which is where the Jewish people first formed as a nation. Their laws, practices, and beliefs were formed thousands of years ago in the ancient land, and even when the Jewish people were forced to leave, their traditions, culture, and memories always related back to their homeland.

ANCIENT KINGDOM

Around 3,000 years ago, in the 10th century BCE, the Israelite tribes formed the Kingdom of Israel, under the first king, Saul. Over the next 100 years, the kingdom split into two: Israel and Judah. Eventually, Israel was conquered by the Assyrians, and Judah was later conquered by the Romans. Many Jews were killed or forced to leave the land.

OVER THE YEARS

Although most Jews were expelled from Israel and Judah by conquering armies and empires, some remained. But even for those far away, their connection to the land never faded. Wherever they are in the world, Jews always pray in the direction of Jerusalem. Jewish festivals are tied to the seasons and agricultural calendar of Israel. Folk songs, stories, and prayers speak of a longing for Eretz Yisrael and Jerusalem, which is also called Zion.

ZIONISM

The Jewish people did not have a homeland for thousands of years, though they longed to return to their ancient land. Zionism is the belief that Jews should be free as a nation in their ancient homeland, Israel. Most of the Jews in the world are zionists.

MODERN COUNTRY

In 1947, the United Nations voted to split the land between the Arabs and Jews who were living there at the time. On May 14, 1948, the state of Israel was founded. Finally, Jewish people were able to live as a free nation in their homeland once more.

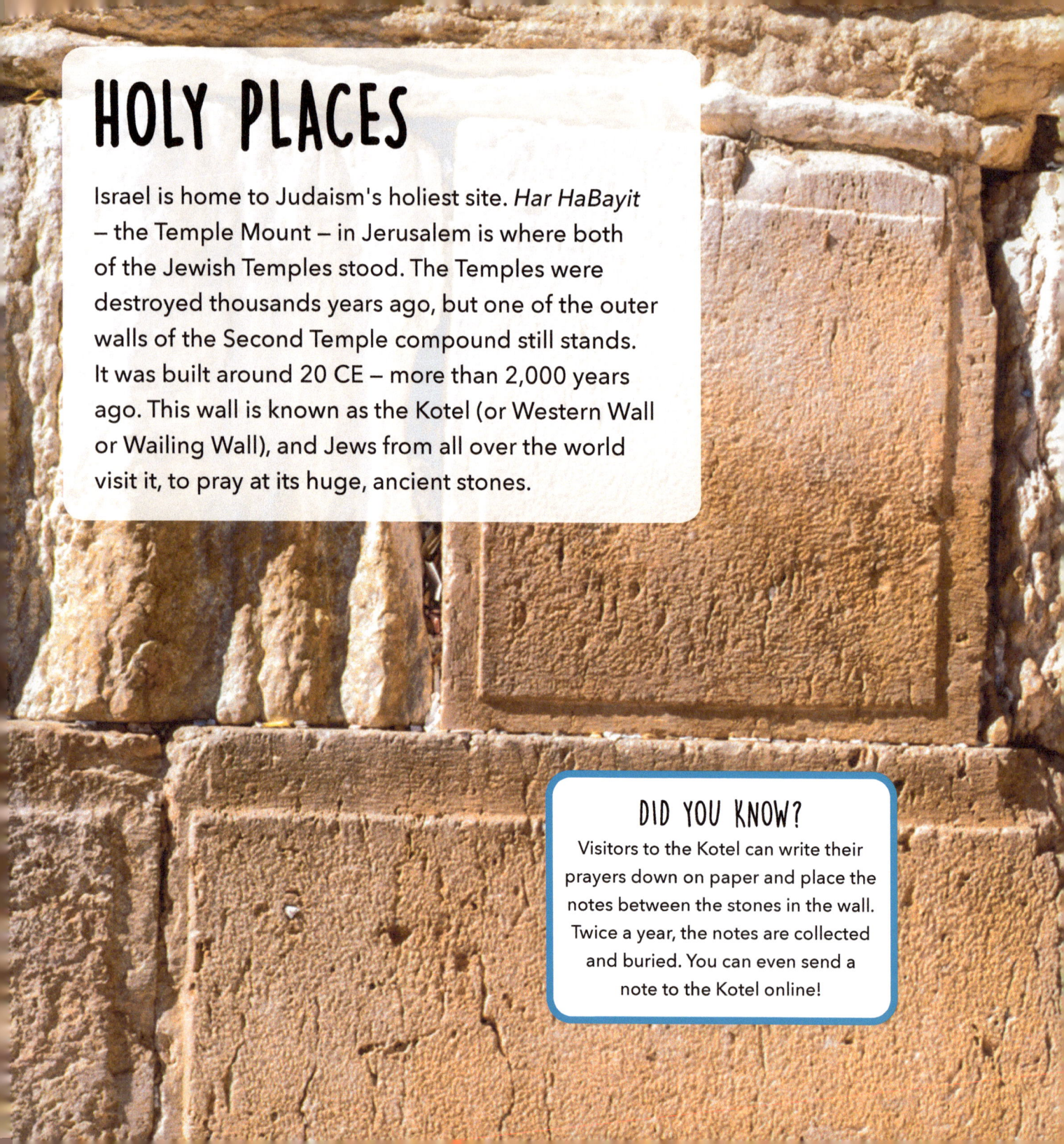

HOLY PLACES

Israel is home to Judaism's holiest site. *Har HaBayit* – the Temple Mount – in Jerusalem is where both of the Jewish Temples stood. The Temples were destroyed thousands years ago, but one of the outer walls of the Second Temple compound still stands. It was built around 20 CE – more than 2,000 years ago. This wall is known as the Kotel (or Western Wall or Wailing Wall), and Jews from all over the world visit it, to pray at its huge, ancient stones.

DID YOU KNOW?
Visitors to the Kotel can write their prayers down on paper and place the notes between the stones in the wall. Twice a year, the notes are collected and buried. You can even send a note to the Kotel online!

HOLY TOMBS
The tombs of biblical figures are generally considered holy sites, as are some tombs of famous rabbis. Jewish people will often travel to them to pray for specific things.

SYNAGOGUE
With no Temple, Jewish people nowadays can connect to God at synagogue. The Torah scrolls are kept in a special cupboard called an "Aron", which is the holiest part of a synagogue.

EVERYWHERE
Jews believe you can connect to God anywhere. While some places might be holier than others, nothing is more holy than speaking to God directly from your heart.

THE JEWISH YEAR

The Jewish year starts with the month of Tishrei. The Hebrew calendar is lunar, so it is based on the cycles of the moon, not the sun. Because of this, Hebrew dates don't match up to the sames dates of the "regular" solar calendar each year. This also means Jewish people have a Hebrew birthday as well as an "English" birthday!

Tishrei (September/October)
ROSH HASHANAH

The Jewish New Year lasts for 2 days and involves a lot of praying and festive meals. A horn called a shofar is blown 100 times each day.

Av (July/August)
TISHA B'AV

A 25-hour fast day to mourn the destruction of the Jewish Temples, and various other tragedies.

Sivan (May/June)
SHAVUOT

The Festival of "Weeks" celebrates the Jewish people receiving the Torah from God at Mount Sinai. It lasts for 2 days (1 in Israel), and involves eating dairy foods, particularly cheesecake!

Iyar (May)
LAG B'OMER

This minor holiday is commonly celebrated with bonfires and picnics. It commemorates the life of an ancient Jewish leader, Shimon bar Yochai, and also marks a day of joy in the 49 days between Passover and Shavuot.

DID YOU KNOW?
To keep the 12 Hebrew months in sync with the seasons, an extra month is added during a leap year. Leap years occur 7 times in a 19-year cycle. How confusing!

Tishrei (September/October)
YOM KIPPUR

A 25-hour fast, Yom Kippur is the Day of Atonement, when Jews reflect on their actions of the past year and ask God for forgiveness. It is the most important of the 6 fast days.

Tishrei (September/October)
SUKKOT

The Festival of Huts, Sukkot lasts for 8 days (7 days in Israel). Jewish people build huts in their gardens to remember how the ancient Jews lived in the desert. Sukkot meals are eaten in these huts.

Kislev (December)
HANUKKAH

The Festival of Lights celebrates how the Jewish people reclaimed their Temple in Jerusalem from the ancient Greeks. A 9-branch candelabra called a hanukkiah is lit every night for 8 nights.

Shvat (January/February)
TU B'SHVAT

A 1-day celebration, this "New Year of the Trees" celebrates nature. Many Jewish people plant trees and eat fruit.

Nisan (March/April)
PASSOVER

This spring festival commemorates how the Jews escaped from slavery in ancient Egypt. It lasts 8 days (7 days in Israel) and starts with a ritual meal called a Seder. On Passover, Jewish people can't eat bread or most other wheat-based products.

Adar (February/March)
PURIM

Purim celebrates how the Jewish people rose up against an enemy who wanted to destroy them in ancient Persia. It lasts one day, and involves dressing up, giving gifts of food and charity, and eating a big feast.

CELEBRATIONS

Jewish kids celebrate their birthdays like most other kids: they might invite friends to a party, open presents, or blow out candles on a cake! But many Jewish celebrations and special occasions also include unique traditions and rituals.

CONGRATULATIONS! To congratulate a Jewish person on a special occasion, say "Mazal Tov!"

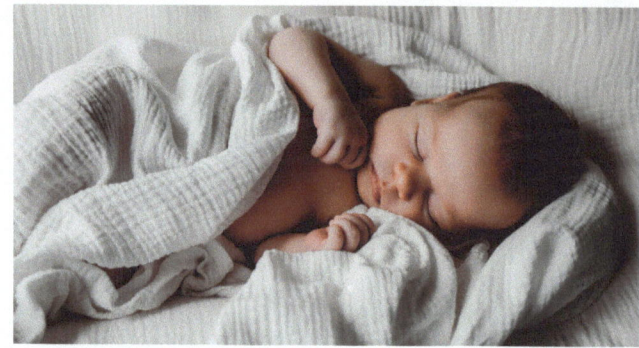

BRIT MILAH

When a baby boy is born, he is named on the eighth day, at a special ceremony called a Brit Milah. Baby girls do not have a Brit, and they can be named as soon as they are born, though many families make a special party for them called a Simchat Bat.

BAR AND BAT MITZVAH

This is a special birthday to celebrate when Jewish children come of age. For girls, this is at age 12 and is called a Bat Mitzvah. For boys, it is at age 13 and is called a Bar Mitzvah. These are usually celebrated at synagogue, where the child reads from the Torah or gives a short speech. Many families also celebrate with an extra special party.

WEDDING

A Jewish wedding takes place under a canopy called a *chuppah*. The bride walks around the groom 7 times, then 7 blessings are recited. Finally, after placing the ring on the bride's finger, the groom smashes a glass, symbolizing the destruction of the Jewish Temple — a reminder that even at our happiest moments, we must remember what we've lost.

TRADITIONAL ASHKENAZI FOOD

CHICKEN SOUP

A chicken broth with vegetables, herbs, and "matzo-ball" dumplings, traditionally eaten Friday night.

CHULENT

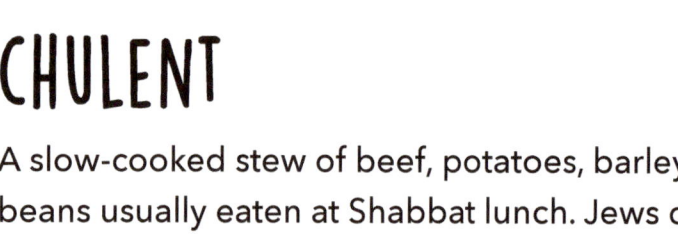

A slow-cooked stew of beef, potatoes, barley, and beans usually eaten at Shabbat lunch. Jews can't cook on Shabbat, so chulent is perfect: you prepare it before Shabbat and it is ready the next day!

BAGELS

Chewy, round bread with a hole in the middle and various toppings, bagels have become known as a Jewish food — especially with a shmear of cream cheese, and lox on top!

BABKA

This sweet, rich cake filled with oozy, sticky chocolate is a firm favorite at kosher bakeries! Perfect as a deslicious Shabbat morning treat.

KUGEL

A baked mixture of grated potatoes, grated onions, and eggs, kugel can be firm or mushy, depending on the recipe! You can also add different vegetables if you like. It tastes savory and warming. Yum!

GEFILTE FISH

Not everyone likes the look of gefilte fish! It's a ball of minced fish flavoured with sugar and salt. The carrot on top is an attempt to make it look a bit better! It tastes good though!

SEPHARDI AND MIZRAHI CUISINE

HAMIN

This is the Sephardi version of chulent, a slow-cooked stew that can be prepared before Shabbat. It uses ingredients common to Jews who lived in Spain, India, and Iraq, such as lamb, rice or chickpeas, and rich, warm spices, including cumin or saffron.

DOLMA

Rice and meat wrapped in the leaves of a grape vine are known as dolma, or vine leaves. They are a popular Sephardi dish. With a lemony flavour, they taste delicious eaten warm and drizzled with raw tahini!

BOUREKAS

Thesed flaky pastries can be stuffed with anything — salty potato, fried mushrooms, spinach and cheese, or even a sweet filling. Mizrahi Jews brought these to Israel and bourekas are now one of the most common Israeli foods. They can be eaten hot or cold for breakfast, lunch, dinner, or just as a tasty snack!

KUBBEH SELEK

Iraqi or Syrian dumplings, known as kubbeh (or kibbe), are made from semolina and stuffed with meat. Kubbeh selek is a classic Mizrahi dish where the kubbeh are cooked in a beet soup that has a tangy, almost sour taste. (*Selek* is the Hebrew word for beets.)

AROUND THE WORLD

There are many Jewish communities across the globe, each with their own culture and history. Let's discover traditions from around the world!

CZECHIA

The Old-New Synagogue in Prague, Czechia, was built in the 13th century. It is the oldest synagogue in continuous use in Europe. These days, around 1,500 Jews live in Prague.

ISRAEL

Israel is home to a truly diverse range of Jewish communities: from Mizrahi, Ashkenazi, and Sephardi to Ethiopian, Indian Bene Israel, African Hebrew Israelites, Yemeni, and of course, Jews whose families have lived there uninterrupted since biblical times.

MOROCCO

Jews have lived in Morocco for thousands of years, and have absorbed many local customs. Before weddings, they have a henna party where the bride and groom's hands are marked with henna dye.

GIBRALTAR

A British territory next to Spain, Gibraltar is famous for its rock and apes. It is also home to a mostly Orthodox Jewish community of around 1,000 people.

JAMAICA
Jews fled to Jamaica following the Spanish Inquisition of 1492. The synagogue in Kingston has a sand floor and its own prayer book, combining Sephardi with liberal/reform prayers.

USA
Bukharian Jews originally settled in and around Uzbekistan and Tajikistan. After the fall of the USSR, many moved to Queens, New York. They are proud of their culture, which they express with delicious food, colorful, richly patterned clothing, and unique traditions.

PERU
The rainforest city of Iquitos is only accessible by plane or boat. There's a tiny Jewish community there. One of their traditions is to hang an Israeli flag over a table throughout the year.

DJERBA
This small island off Tunisia is home to one of the oldest Jewish communities in the world. They practice many ancient traditions, including blowing a shofar (a ram's horn) from a rooftop on Fridays to remind everyone that Shabbat is coming.

AZERBAIJAN
A mixture of Ashkenazi, Sephardi, and Mizrahi Jews live in Azerbaijan. The majority moved from Persia, and are known as Mountain Jews. They speak a language called Juhuri, or Judeo-Tat.

JEWISH OBJECTS

These are some common objects that may be found in a Jewish home. Many are passed down as family heirlooms, or bought as special gifts.

Tefillin, worn on the head and arm during prayer by boys once they reach Bar Mitzvah age

Shofar, a horn blown on Rosh Hashanah

Shabbat candlesticks, lit to welcome in Shabbat

Two-handled cup for ritual hand washing before a meal

Kiddush cup for wine at Shabbat and festive meals

Hanukkiah, lit on Hanukkah

Seder plate for Passover

Mezuzah, hung on every doorpost

DID YOU KNOW?
The "Shema" prayer that is written on scrolls inside mezuzahs and tefillin is the same prayer Jews say before bed. The first line says: "Hear, oh Israel, HaShem is our God, HaShem is One."

First published in Great Britain in 2024
by TELL ME MORE Books

Text copyright ©2024 Shari Black
Design copyright ©2024 Shari Black

ISBN: 978-1-917200-33-2

Picture credits: Thanks to Adobe Stock; Maciej Swulinski; Jan Cassalette at Unsplash; ChameleonsEye, Edel Mar, Denphumi, George Kurgin, Grafvision, Jinjo0222988, John Theodor, Leah P, LuVo, Maren Wischnewski, Monkey Business Images, Pang3D, PhotoObjects.net, Pixelshot, RafiG770, Roxana_Ro, Ruslan Dashinsky, StefaNikolic, Sterling_photo, Tomertu, Tovfla, TzahiV, Vanitjan, and Yrabota.

All rights reserved. Without limiting the rights under the copyright reserved above, no part of this publication may be reproduced, stored in, or introduced into a retrieval system, or transmitted, in any form, or by any means (electronic, mechanical, photocopying, recording or otherwise), without the prior written permission of the copyright owner.

WWW.TELLMEMOREBOOKS.COM

www.ingramcontent.com/pod-product-compliance
Lightning Source LLC
Chambersburg PA
CBHW040020130526
44590CB00036B/40